CONTENTS

Introduction		
On Transcribing Dialect		5
I	Identification	9
II	Well	12
III	T'Good Earth	13
IV	Luv, Bob	15
V	Ah Might, Mebbe, It All Depens, Ah'll See	17
VI	T'Boss's Philosophy	19
VII	To Mi' Son John	21
VIII	To Mi Dawter	25
IX	Redundancy	30
X	Leukin' Back	32
XI	Skeulin	34
XII	T'Pig An Curran Ceeak	36
XIII	Wartime Memories	37
XIV	T'Buffet Supper	40
XV	Diggin	42
XVI	T'Beeat Group	44
XVII	T'Laund-er-ette	46
XVIII	Thowts After A Pain Management Course	49
XIX	Mi Targets	51
Glossary		52

ACKNOWLEDGEMENTS

These poems might never have appeared in print had it not been for the nagging of a few close friends and the help they gave when it came to the crunch. I have my daughter to thank – Janet Wren, and John and Peggy Troll who did the typing and delved into mysteries unknown to me in the innards of Word Processors. Then there is Terry Cluderay of Hawes who doctored the proofs and got them through the Press. I am grateful to the Lakeland and Yorkshire Dialect Societies for the opportunity to speak dialect at their meetings; and last but not least to the many who remain my friends after much patient listening to me.

Jane Horner Smith

INTRODUCTION

The following poems were written over a period of years as a purely personal expression of intimate, private feelings and are now being published only after the persistent promptings of friends who recognised not only their literary merit but also their value as social history covering a lifestyle that has passed out of practical experience. The directness of statement and immediacy of their appeal is due in part to the dialect in which they are written and which was the only tongue the author heard or spoke during her formative years.

Jane Smith was born on the eve of World War I in the Wapentake of Gilling West to John Horner Carter, a joiner born and bred by the banks of the Swale and knowing only the dialect of that dale, and Beatrice from Well near Bedale. Dialect was the natural speech in their home and at Gilling West Elementary School from where Jane, a scholarship girl, went to Richmond High School for Girls at the age of eleven. There, and later at the City of Leeds Training College for Teachers, she became bilingual but never lost her love of dialect and never ceased to use it when the occasion suited – as, for example, at meetings of The Yorkshire Dialect Society. She taught Art and Craft in Barnsley for four years before moving to the Headship of East Cowton in 1936. There she met and, in 1941, married Robert Smith of Cocklebury Farm. She gave up teaching and farmed with her husband in Great Smeaton and then in Cumbria until his untimely death in 1967. "Luv Bob" is a kind of memorial to him and twenty-five years of happiness.

Some dialect verse depends for its appeal solely upon the dialect. Take that away and the interest has gone. Others have intrinsic merit but, because of the transliteration, present the reader with so much difficulty that full appreciation is impossible. Here, it may be thought, neither is true. With the help of a short glossary most readers will find no obstacle to understanding; and even if written in standard English, though much would be lost, the poetry would remain. That is nothing strange to those who have known the author over many years, aware of her indomitable spirit through mental anguish and the physical pain of a long disablement, and of her unceasing search for personal enrichment. Her life, though in a chair for the most part, is fuller at seventy-five than that of many a younger and fitter person. Still a member of both the Yorkshire and Cumbria Dialect Societies, in whose journals some of her poems have been published, she keeps up her lifelong art and craft activities – painting, spinning, weaving; and at the age of seventy-four she became a graduate of the Open University. Small wonder, then, that with the 'gift of tongues' a poetry sequence such as 'Luv Bob' should emerge.

Terence M. Cluderay.

ON TRANSCRIBING DIALECT

Dialect is not and never was a written language. Perhaps the nearest definition of it is 'the way people used to speak in a specified area'; but that is both too much and too little. It ignores the fact that some people still speak it though they are now usually 'bilingual'. More importantly it lumps both slang and slovenly speech with a local vocabulary, with intonation and with pronunciation. It could also be thought to imply that areas can be clearly specified whereas there is a considerable overlap. Nevertheless it will serve; and it does stress the essential oral aspect.

Attempts to reproduce dialect in writing have no long history. There was very little of it before Robert Burns. Tennyson tried it in the 19th century with but small success. William Barnes, poet and clergyman who died in 1861, was a pioneer in the study of dialect – in his case of Dorset; but it was not until our own times that it became a 'group' interest with the foundation of societies and the proliferation of a literature in and about dialect – largely, though not solely, verse. It was then that solutions were sought to the problems of transliteration. In addressing myself to these I am concerned primarily with Yorkshire dialects.

First it must be admitted there is no completely satisfactory solution – not even if phonetic symbols were used and everyone understood them. Quite apart from the unreality and ugliness of such a procedure, how does one indicate the glottal stop? Probably the most well-known example of this is the phrase "Up fer t'cup" where it is represented, conventionally, by "t'" which means nothing to a person who has not heard a Yorkshireman speak and who, in any case, cannot achieve the sound. It may, indeed, mean nothing even to a Yorkshireman who will sometimes pronounce the "t" when he sees it written – especially before a vowel or aitch, though he would never do so when speaking. The usual solution is to use spelling variations e.g. "fer" for "for", "tha" for "thee" or "thou"; but these are not unequivocal. The preposition "to" might be any one of the following; "ta, te, ti, tu, tuh, ter, tiv, tev, tew or t'". The last one is inadmissable as it would be confused with the glottal stop and one could have "Is ta gahn t't' pikchers?" in the West Riding for "Are you going to the cinema?" Similarly the length and breadth of vowel sounds cannot be fully conveyed either by spelling variants (often by doubling the vowel) or by using quantity marks. The northern "brass" is not conveyed by "brahss" or "braass" or by putting a long or a short mark over the vowel. With how many "a"s should one transliterate the West Yorkshire "make" – "May-ayk" "Father" is pronounced in the West Riding with a flattened broad 'a' or a flattened short 'a' – if that means anything to the general reader; elsewhere it may be "feyther" or "fether". The personal pronoun "I" will in the West Riding generally be "A" (short "a") but, emphasised it becomes "Ah". For example: "Az goin' aht." (or "Az gahin oot" or "Az bahn out" – all of them meaning "I'm going out") whereas: "Ahz goin' aht even of thahz stayin' in". In North Yorkshire "meeak" will serve for "make" but the actual sound is somewhere between that and "mayuk". The problem is twofold: the writer's – how to transliterate, and the reader's – how to interpret. Nor is the latter confined to readers outside the territory. I know one octogenarian who cannot speak anything but dialect (which, by definition therefore, is not dialect to him) and can read only standard English. When confronted with a passage that was a transliteration of his own spoken language he could not read a word.

Consistency would seem to be imperative. To vacillate between "ti" and "te" would make the reader think different sounds were indicated. Unfortunately thy sometimes do, e.g. a Wensleydale dialect speaker will mix "ti", "tiv" and "tev" – to name but a few! Further complications arise from the many different vowel sounds that will be changed in speech to the one sound. The dissyllable "eea", for example, can replace at least seven different vowel sounds (long "a", long "o", short "o", "oo", "ee", short "e", short "i") but not invariably. Around Simonstone (or Simmison) at the Southern end of The Buttertubs Pass, the word "stone" could be either "stane" or "steean" – the former being the normal Swaledale pronunciation and the latter Wensleydale. At this point the boundary between the two dales is about one mile. Note, however, in both places "fourteen pun is yan ston"! And what is one to "mayuk" (or in the West Riding "mek") of a dialect that pronounces "weak" "wake" and "wake" "weeak"; or will leave out an initial "y" as in "ears" for 'years' but put one in where there is none as in "yackers" for "acres".

Omissions and abbreviations, normally indicated by an apostrophe, are more often examples of slovenly speech than of either slang or dialect. Most of us clip our words in conversation so that it is necessary, when transliterating, to be able to indicate the curtailment. "I drava" for "I would rather" is not, need it be said, dialect. On the other hand "gang" meaning "to go" is genuine dialect and not a corruption of "going" as, however, the cockney "ga'in" clearly is. "Gi'en" for "Given" is not dialect but slovenly speech. The glottal stop is an ommission of a whole word – "the" – and might better be expressed solely by an apostrophe or, better, by some neutral sign such as an asterisk – except that that would send people looking for a footnote. There is a tendency for apostrophes to break out like a measles rash on a page of dialect. One should, therefore either omit the more obvious ones such as the final consonant in "walking" and the medials in "getting" etc. or spell out the word in full. Ambiguity needs to be avoided in, say, using "an" without the apostrophe for "and" and when it could be the indefinite article "an". However, in West Riding the conjunction is more likely to be reduced to the middle letter only – "n", whereas in Wensleydale it will more often than not be "en". Similarly with the broad "u" – which is, perhaps, the one Northern sound a Southerner thinks he knows. There are in fact several shades of them but none is adequately represented by using either an umlaut or a wavey line above it. On the whole it is best left alone for readers to make what they can of it.

Local turns of phrase are usually a mixture of slovenly speech and dialect with a bit of slang sometimes thrown in (the borderline between slang and dialect being often blurred) but they form an integral part of translating into dialect as distinct from transliterating. Anyone can transliterate but only a speaker of the dialect can translate English into it. For example, knowledge of psalm 127 would enable one to understand "t'job's nowt" in James Alderson's translation; "Tryen ta put a hoose wi'oot t'Lord's help – t'job's nowt"; but only someone familiar with Wensleydale speech would have used it, for only such a one would have known that the expression is a common one for "We're wasting out time, we're getting nowhere". It is undoubtedly a "dialect expression" and it contains the glottal stop as well as the dialect use of "naught" – now generally obsolete or poetic, but here in the slang form "nowt"). Incidentally, how many who had never heard "nowt" pronounced would get it right from the spelling? In parts of West Yorkshire it rhymes with "owt" whereas in North Yorkshire the sound is more like "nawoot" spoken quickly.

Transliteration (an editor's concern) and translation (the author's) are both involved in the pieces that follow as also are dialect, slang and slovenly speech. Consistency has been aimed at if not always achieved. A proliferation of apostrophes has been eschewed. This is easier in North than in West Yorkshire as the former is less slovenly. Aspirates are sounded more often in the North than in the West, so are final and medial consonants.

When all's said and done it remains true that the only way one could get the best out of these pieces would be to follow with the eye whilst listening to a local saying them. This, however, is easily achieved for tapes are becoming perhaps more prevalent than books but it is less easy nowadays to find someone who can speak dialect. A tape of these poems has been made.

Terence M. Cluderay

I IDENTIFICATION

Nicholson, Scurrah, Lofthouse,
  Horner, Carter,
What a mixture!
  Ah'll put misell i' t'picture.
Who's Ah?
  Nicholson cam fra t'Isle o' Skye
Ti Yorkshire's plain,
  Wurked wi' might an' main,
An' wedded t'dawter
  Of t'blacksmith fra Well.
T'Scurrahs med ploos,
  Shod t'osses,
Sharpened t'socks
  Ti ton t'furrows
Of t'clay saddened land,
  Fer it wurn't fit
Ti summer a teeafit.
  T'farmers bred flocks
Of Massam sheep
  On t'cultivated soil.
Night an' day thu'd toil.
  T'wimmen seun fun
Eut 'ow ti card t'lang stapled wool,
  Ti bi spun
An' med inti woosit cloth.
  They wur loth
Ti sail ti furrin lands
  Far ower t'watter.
Ti emigrate, intigrate,
  An' 'appen, tempt thur fate.

Lofthouse, a titled Lord,
  Wur impoverished, bored
Wi' t'Irish sward.
  T'tatie famine
Ed med 'im cum in
  Ti till broad yackers
Of Mowbray's Vale.
  "E. Lofthouse, aged fowerteen"
Is stitched in t'finest
  Crosses ivver seen
On t'sampler.
  Shu's mi Grannie twice ower,
An' wur born i' 1804.
  Varra seun t'brood grew an' grew,
An' t'genes
  Of t'family spreead
Ti Swadil's scenes.
  Theear, Tibby Horner of Wathgill,
T'gran'dawter of Lofthouse
  Fra Coverdil,
Ran away to espouse
  Gooarge Carter,
T'joiner fra Down'um,
  An' Ah gat mah neeam.

This pedigree,
  Related by me,
Shows ut t'breed
  'll 'appen succeed.
T'present generation
  Wi' t'computerisation
Of t'scientific age,
  'll manage
Ti weather
  Onny trade recession,
Or economic depression.

Soa, Ah noa why
Ah's I.

Jane Horner Smith (nee Carter)
Granddaughter of
Jane and James Nicholson (nee Lofthouse)
formerly of Oak Tree Farm, Langwith
Well
Bedale
Yorks.
and of
Tibby and George Carter
(nee Horner of Wathgill)
formerly of Downholme
Richmond
Yorks
Tibby was the granddaughter of Lofthouse
from Coverdale

II WELL

(Nr. Bedale, Yorks.)

WELL, neeamed someweear
  In Australia's bare
Country.
  Nicholsons, great-great uncles
Of mine,
  Went to divine
Watter.
  T'azel twig browt lots o' brass in
T'bachelors left neither kith nor kin,
  Only a neeam
That's t'seeam
  As "WELL".
Mi grannie Jane, allus oped thu'd sail
  Y'ham, wi' t'brass.
'Appen it's nobbut a teeal.

III T'GOOD EARTH

Farmin's likely i' mi blood,
  So it wur natural ut Ah sud
Wed a farmer, yah Bob Smith.
  Ah thowt abowt t'lang time sin
Mi grannie Carter of Wathgill ed been
  Courtin' ur Gooarge i' Swadil.
Laikin' i' t'orchard wi' merry shout,
  Peltin' yan anuther wi' laal apples,
Thu'd soon been fun eut.
  Plucky laal Tibby at deead o' night
Astride a trusty Gallowa'
  Galloped ti Coverdil i' desperate plight.
Shu'd gitten 'ur own way!

Fooak sed: "Nowt pairs 'em
  Like thu pair thursells."
Ah thowt: "It all depens
  On t'lad an' t'lass.
Ah'll wurk mi fingers ti t'bone,
  Ti addle brass an' pay t'bank loan."
Ah wur onnything fra t'hind ti t'clerk
  An' Ah scratted on fra dawn ti dark.

Thu wur t'cauves ti sarra, t'ens ti feed,
  T'sheep ti chase eut o' t'maiden seed.
T'milk to sile, t'oss ti catch,
  An' t'straw ti pull fer t'thatch,
T'cocks ti mek wi' a 'andy fork,
  T'ducks ti plooat an' t'sheep ti mawk,
T'bands ti tie when opennin' eut,
  T'ceus ti be driven wi' monny a cleut
T'ay ti loaden on ti t'cart
  An' t'pigs ti mark fer t'mart.

T'men could yut five meals a day,
  "Thoo's married a lot o' wark,"
Was all t'auld uns 'ud say.
  Weeal, wi' two 'ands (Ah cud ev done wi ten)
Ah tried ti feed gurt leatherin' men,
  Wi' tea-ceeaks, pasties, courtin' ceeak,
By gow, Ah seun lurnt ti meeake
  Yuvin bottom an'curran ceeak,
Yorkshire puddin' an' all mek
  Of breead, scones, butter an' cheese.
Onnything ut 'ud pleease
  T'Boss, an' fill em up
Ti t'throttle.

When t'wurk were done, Ah luved ti stare
  At t'laal fooal nuzzling up ti t'mare
At t'ripple o' t'wind passing ower t'grass
  An' 'ark ti t'prattle o' mi bonny laal lass.
T'joy o' seeing t'swallers flitter
  An' t'newly shot barley gleam an' glitter,
T'clocker 'ugging ur chippin' eggs
  An' t'wall eyed sheep dog 'ut begs
Fer t'warmth o' t'kitchen mat,
  Aye, mi art aches fer mooer ner all that.

T'Boss 'es gone;
  Mi bairns 'ev fligged;
Ah've done mi whack.
  'Appen t'next clutch 'll
Gan ageean ti t'land an' till
  T'good earth yance mooer,
As Tibby did lang time afooer.

IV LUV, BOB

Mi darlin' Lass,
  Ah'd better finnd taam
Ti drop Thoo a line.
  Ah've nowt ti say
Only ut second crop of 'ay's
  stacked up ti t'easins.

Ah's pleeasin Thoo wi t'letter,
  But Ah'd be much better
Oppenin eut t'corn,
  Ready fer t'binder
Termorrer morn.

Ah thinks of Thoo in t'early dawn,
  When all's peace an quiet,
Afooer t'riot
  Of feedin taam.
Judy's slinkin off efter a rabbit,
  Insteead of fetchin'
T'ceus in fer milkin'.

Ah've cleeaned eut t'stell.
  (Ah ope Thoo's weeal.)
T'awd ceu Nell's
  Gitten a effer cawf.
Ah've just yutten awf
  A pund of 'am.
Nowt matters
  When Thoo's nut at y'ham.

T'faller field's been plooed,
  An it's fit ageean fer ooats.
Thoo knaws Ah dooats
  On Thoo.

Ow's t'bairns?
  Ah ope it rains,
Fer t'watter in t'pond is varra low,
  An teeamin rain wad mek t'girss grow.
Thoo'll likely knaw
  Ut Cliff Watson's gitten wed.
Ah've bowt misell some curran' breead.

Ah's thinner
  An longin fer a Sunday dinner.
Mi trouser knees is eut,
  Thoo's a dab 'and at stitchin on a clout.
Thoo'll mebbe git a freet
  When we meet,
Ah's sike a seet,
  An leuk just like a gipsy,
But it's nobbut t'arvest meun,
  T'sun an t'smell o' t'stubble
Ut meks mi breun an tipsy.
  Ah doan't tek t'trouble
Ti bi spick an span
  When Thoo's nut at y'ham.

By gum it's yat
  Ah've ed ti weear
Mi awd straw 'at.
  Ah think thu'll be a thunner storm.
T'ceus ev brokken inter t'corn.
  Ah'll ev ti end mi letter.
Drat this orked pen,
  A stob
Fra' t'awd brown 'en
  Wad ev been better.
Luv, Bob.

V AH MIGHT, MEBBE, IT ALL DEPENS, AH'LL SEE

"Will ter bi gaain ti market terday?"
  Ah sed to t'Boss
As he lowsed eut t'oss,
  "It's been mizzlin an t'ay
Weean't bi fit afooer neun.
  Ah'll seun do mi shoppin,
While Thoo's swappin
  Teeals at t'mart."
"Ah'll see. T'ceu's springin,
  T'sew's a brimmin,
T'cauf's gitten t'euse,
  T'mare's cast yan of ur shoes.
It's no use,
  Thoo's mun stop at y'ham,
An mek thi gooseburry jam."

"Please,
  Tek mi ti t'village,
Yer can call at t'garidge.
  Ah'll buy cheese,
Meeat, yest an breead,
  An Ah's cleean eut o' sewing threead.
We'll fetch t'sacks fra t'station,
  Pick up t'eggs fer incubation,
Tek t'cutter bar ti t'smiddy,
  Posst t'subsidy fer t'cauves."

"Nay, Ah's ower thrang,
  T'beease ev gitten wrang,
T'bull's on t'rampage.
  Thoo'll etter manidge.
We can yut fried 'am

An puddin boiled in a cleut.
Ah reely owt
Ti stop at y'ham."

"Duster want a ride ti Corn 'ill Farm?"
Ah thowt "Ah can ton on mi charm,
Weear mi new togs,
Git eut o' these clogs."
T'Boss's enthusiasm wur nobbut lukewarm,
An he answered wi' a leuk of alarm,
"Ah's only gaain ti borrow some socks,
Fer t'new 'uns is brokken on t'ard rocks,
Ah reely deean't knaw
Whether t'car 'ull go,
Fer it's nobbut dicky.
Dang it, t'engine's tricky,
An it weean't start,
Ah could mebbe yoke up t'cart.
Noa? Then we'll etter stop at y'ham."

Amang this frustration,
Ah thinks on of t'occasion,
When stannin' at t'altar
Ah thowt t'Boss ud falter,
An' say, "Ah might, mebbe,
It all depens, Ah'll see."
Ah gat t'shock of mi life,
Fer neu Ah's 'is wife.
He said "Ah will",
Nut, "Wait until
Ah gaa back y'ham
Ti fassen up t'ram."
Or "'Odd on, Ah's nut quite sure
Whether Thoo's reely t'reight yan,
Ah'd mebbe better stop at y'ham."

VI T'BOSS'S PHILOSOPHY

Reight in t'middle of t'winter's blast
  Ah fun ut cooal wadn't last eut.
T'Boss said,
  "Weel, doant fash thisell.
Remember t'calamity
  When t'milk cam back las' September? *
T'ceus fancied a change o' diet
  An yut seuwer apples on t'quiet.
Ah've chopped deun t'danged crab apple tree.
  An if Thoo's cawd
Git od o' yon cross-cut saw
  We'll etter bon mooer an mooer
Green wood afooer t'thow.
  Thoo'll seun warm thisell up, lass,
An Ah'll seeave a mint o' brass."

While catchin' a duck
  Ah missed t'gurt wopper
An cam a reeal belly flopper
  Tummlin reight amang t'muck.
T'men neely ed ti dig
  Mi eut of t'mig.
T'Boss said in 'is dry way,
  "Doant fash thisell,
We'll etter throw Thoo in ti t'pond
  An scrub Thoo deun wit' yard broom."
'E leuked mi up an deun –
  Thoo'll nut dreun.
Thur's nobbut room
  Fer Thoo an t'duck
In t'watter."

* "T'milk cam back" – The churns of milk were returned from the Dairy at Northallerton, because the crab apples had caused the milk to sour!

Laitin t'nest of t'turkey 'en
  Ut ud laid away
I' t'orchard, t'nettles, t'staggarth –
  Wheear?
Ah'd fergitten ut t'dough
  Wad grouw an grouw.
Thur wur mooer
  Peeast than ud fill t'pancheon,
Ah fun it ud spreead
  All ower t'flooer.
Neu, spoilt breead
  Wadn't feead
T'Boss,
  Nut ti mention
T'ungry men.
  "Doant fash thisell, lass,
Thoo mun ton us all eut ti girss."

Thur's monny a crisis to feeace alone,
  Ah've ti keep up appearances an' nivver mooan,
T'battery's flat, t'tyre's worn,
  T'fire weeant light
An thur's t'plight
  Of a busted pipe.
Ah've lurnt ti change t' plug,
  An lug
T'gurt shoppin baskets y'ham.
  Ah try ti do t'best Ah can.
Offens Ah fergits mi specs,
  Can't finnd mi keys.
T'dog leead gits tangelled reund mi knees,
  Ah gits misell i' sike a stew
Ah ardlins knaw whativver ti deu.
  Then Ah sits misell deun
An fra far away
  Ah 'ears t'Boss say,
In 'is quiet way,
  "Doant fash thisell, lass,
It'll pass."

VII TO MI' SON JOHN

Thoo was a bonny
  Laal babby,
But even then
  Mebbe
Awd Nick
  'Ed gitten od of thoo,
Or else t'fost sign
  Of t'inventive mind
Wur apparent,
  Fer thoo'd been an' gone
An' brokken thi pram,
  Afooer thoo could walk
Or talk.

T'mechanical urge
  Surged i thi' 'eead,
Thoo nivver feared
  T'din of t'tractors,
T'threshers, t'engines.
  Ah call ter mind
When thi Dad 'ud finnd
  'ud t'tractor wadn't start,
Fer thoo'd stolen t'flooat,
  An tekken t'engine apart.

Thoo'd a mania
  Fer undoin nuts, an' screws.
Yance, it wur plain
  'ut two 'undred gallons of paraffin
'ed gone deun t'drain.
  T'news spreead like wildfire
That thi dad wes t'sire
  Of t'Divil 'isell!

T'sewin' machine
  Wur t'next on t'list.
Wi' thi laal fist
  Thoo unscrewed
All t'nobs.
  Thur wur bits an' bobs
All ower t'flooer.
  It wur years afooer
Ah gat t'screws ter fit,
  Nut ter mention
T'tension,
  Which nivver wur t'seeam ageean.

Gran' father's watch
  Wur noa match
Fer thi cunnin'
  Wi' a good will
(An' unerrin' skill)
  Thoo disembowelled
T'treasured eirloom,
  Ran inter t'room,
Shoutin'
  "Tick, Tock, Nanna!"
In a manner
  Full of confidence,
An' common sense.
  Thoo'd done t'job reight weel
An' left nobbut
  T'empty, silver shell.

Fost car we 'ed
  Wur ARJ eight double yan,
Noo thi Dad med
  It plain,
Said ageean an' ageean,
  "Ah'll tan thi backside
If thoo gans inside

T'car."
But thoo wicked laal lad
Tricked thi Dad,
An' from t'eutside,
In a clever manner
Reely put t'spanner
In t'wurks,
Fillin' up t'tank wi sand an' gravel.
Ivver efter we'd ter travel
Up t' 'ills in reverse,
Wi' monny a curse.

Soa as t'years passed on,
Ah'd finnd
'ut t'enquirin' mind
Of mi son
Lapped up t'radio, t'motor bike,
An' sike like.
Thoo could allus
Git t'tractor ter start,
An' tek part
In t'maintenance of t'farm.
Thoo'd lend a 'and,
Build owt fra sand
An' mortar,
Fix t'slates on t'roof,
'Tend ter t' 'oof
Of t'leeam ceu;
Fettle a cauf pen
An' then
Build up t'wall gaps.

Noo thoo's fligged fra y'ham.
  Wurk on t'farm is ower an' done.
T'dark neets
  Of cannels an' t'lamps is ower.
An' under t'breet lights
  Men 'ull destroy t'weeds,
An' t'pests,
  Ter satisfy t'needs
Of t'best farmin' skills.
  'Appen it's a cure fer all ills,
But who's ter test
  T'rest
Of t'damage 'ut's done?
  T'battle of destruction
Is ower an' won.
  It's up ter sike
Scientists as thoo
  Ter finnd t'solution,
An' seeave mankind
  Fra its own destruction.

VIII TO MI DAWTER

Shu's a May kittlin *
  An' shu owter been dreuned.
T'fost thing Ah fund
  Wus that 'ur 'eead wur creuned
Wi' a thick black thatch.
  Shu'd yell fer 'ours,
An' ud allus fratch,
  Fer shu didn't like t'leuk
Of us strange 'uman fooak.

T'geslings, t'fluffy chicks,
  T'new-born puppies, an' t'laal lambs
Wur 'ur joy.
  Shu'd let t'coy
Witters perch on 'ur eead,
  An' nivver feared
T'awd steg.
  Shu'd stand fer 'ours
Mareuned on t'tractor trailer,
  At t'mercy o' Percy —
A gurt fierce turkey.

At lambin' time,
  Shu'd keep watch
An' go round t'sheep
  At t'crack o' dawn,
Spottin' t'new born lambs.
  Noa savage gull ner wily fox
'Ud ivver engage
  Wi' 'is prey, when Girlie
Wur on t'rampage.

* According to country lore, May Kittens never thrive and should therefore be drowned.

Shu'd watch t'young swallers
  Peep ower t'edge o' t'nest,
An' finnd t'best
  Spot in t' 'ay moo
Ti yut 'ur stolen currans,
  An' 'ide fra Muther
An' 'ur big brother.

T'laal lass
  'Ud ton ower 'ur brass,
When shu 'eeard t'fost cuckoo's call
  I' Spring,
Ter bring
  Good Luck.
Shu could allus spy
  T'skylark soarin' 'igh
Nobbut a speck in t'clear blue sky.

Skeulin, meant
  Lessons lurnt at Waberthwaite.
Carefree days,
  An' playgreund ways
Of singin' monny a song;
  "T'Farmer's in 'is Den".
"Ooats an' Beans an' Barley Grow".
  T'Inspectors ud gaze,
An murmur,
  "An Idyllic Phase!"
Nay, nobbut a natural way
  Of tekkin reut in t'land.
Battlin ageeanst t'weather,
  T'wind, t'rain, t'snaw an' t'mist,
Shu lurnt ter bi as tough
  As leather.

T'gurt Big Skeul,
  Meant
New skills, new beuks,
  New leuks,
'Air styles,
  An' wiles.
Shu grew up
  Ti a mature way
Of evin ur own say
  Abeut a career
With a veneer of sophistication.
  But Girlie
Ud allus bi reight glad
  Ti 'elp ur Dad,
Build a wall gap,
  Or 'ap up
T'beease at neet,
  Shu'd wesh eggs, fork 'ay,
An ed a special way
  Wi pet lambs, weeakly cauves,
An' pooly chicks.

Then she fligged fra y'ham
  Wus engulfed
In London's bustle,
  An' all t'ectic 'ustle
Of student life.
  Thur's a reeal tussle
Fer survival
  Under t'eeaves in a bed-sitter
In Hampsteead.
  Shu teuk ur 'euk
Ti tek a leuk
  At foreign lands.
Shu cam back y'ham
  Fra North, South, East, and West.
Shu's wed,

Gitten a laal lass
An med ur nest
I' London.

Shu'll need all t'memories
Shu can muster.
Ah wunder
Does shu remember
'Ow shu yuster
Tell t'awd rhyme,
"Nimmy, Nimmy Nack,
Which 'and will yer tack?"
An' Ah'd oppen mi eyes
Ter t'surprise
Of t'fost snawdrops,
Or t'yellow primroses
Shu'd fund at t'edge of' t'beck.

Shu'd mek
Daisy chains,
Garlandin ur pet lamb,
Rosy Posy.
Shu'll call ti mind
T'sunsets an' t'copper skies,
Ower t'Isle o'Man,
An' wekkenin' up ti finnd
T'lonnin blocked wi' drifted snaw,
An' t'fell wind ut ud blaw an' blaw
Fer three lang days, aye mooer.
Gossamer threeads stretched eut
On blackthorn boughs,
Beeaded wi' mist in t'early morn,
T'mad March 'ares,
An' t'foxes' lairs
On t'fell,
T' stillness of neet,
T'cock's craw

At t'fost streeak o' dayleet,
Contented ceus munchin,
T'job o'bunchin'
Daffodils fer sale on Muther's day,
T'acrid stink o' byre, 'ull an stye,
T'sweet smell of new mown 'ay,
T'girss's urge fer growth
Efter t'soft warm rain i' May,
Ceus croppin' lush green girss,
A dewdrop's sparkle ut ud pass
In a momentary flash,
An t'mad dash
Fer shelter in a thunner storm,
T'stillness of neet
And t'fust streeak o'dayleet,
These are t'memories
Shu'll recall
Whativver shu does,
Weearivver shu roams,
Fer thur part of 'ur
Deep deun in 'ur booans.

IX REDUNDANCY

Nobbut t'fireless 'earth an' t'geeable end
  Mark t'spot wheear t'Carter family could mend
An mek onny ilk o' carts,
  Wi' spokes riven fra' yak, naffs of awm,
Fellies of esh, grown i' different parts
  O' Swadil.

Beams sawn in t'pit an' shaped wi' t'adze
  Wur med wi' sike care,
Thu'd last un weear
  A undred yeears, aye mooer.

"A poor wukman allus blames 'is tools",
  Mi father said, an' "Fools
An' bairns should nivver see a job alf done".
  T'joiner's pride was in a job weeal done.
A winder or a dooer wur med ter last
  Ti keep out t'blast
Of t'winter's storm.

T'corner cupboard, t'rocking chair,
  T'fower posster bed an' t'kitchen press,
T'auld bellesis an' t'creddle
  T'blanket kist an' t'fiddle,
Proud possessions of monny a farm
  Nivver cam ti' onny arm,
An' are wuth mooer cash
  Ner all t'modern trash.

T'forestry 'll plant spruce, filling
  T'land wi' regimented lines
Like sowjers, drilling.
  "Laminated" is t'latest fashion
Med i' factories, wi' nobbut a ration
  O' t' pure wood.

So t'shavings, t'chisel, t'plane an t'ammer
  Aye, Nazareth's wurkshop, are redundant
In a scientific age, abundant
  I' larning, brass an' t'clamour
O' machines.
  Only t'ruins and t'antiques remain
Of an age 'ut wur mebbe, sane.

X LEUKIN' BACK

Ah can think on
  Of t'Peace Tea
An t'bonnin of t'effigee
  Of Kaiser Bill
On Richmond's 'ill.
  It's nobbut a memory
Mekkin tea
  At Barnsla
Fer t'unger marchers
  Fra Jarrow
An t'parties in t'narrer
  Streets fer t'Silver Jubilee
Of Gooarge an' Mary.
  Well,
T'abdication of mi pin up boy
  An t'relief of t'nation
At t'Coronation
  Of t'next relation's
As clear as a bell.
  We organised t'Peace Pledge
An walked eut t'Pennine Way
  On t'edge o' t'moors.
"Cowton in the clay"
  Neu, Ah cam that way
Just a year o' mooer
  Afoor t'second world war.
It's nobbut a cock stride
  Sin Ah wur up ti t'ees
Wi' evacuees
  'Elpin ti save t'nation
Fra' 'Itler's vexation.
  Then Cummerlan's scene.
Ah've been
  At Bootle, Muncaster,

Waberthwaite an'
  Millom skeuls
Fer nigh on thirty years.
  Ah've been kept on t'op!
Listened ti t'top
  O' t'Pops
To keep in tune
  Wi' Pat, Milly or June.
Ah've admired t'curls,
  Put wi' t'smiles
An t'wiles
  Of t'thurd form girls.
T'lads 'ev called mi "Awd Ma Smith"
  Or "Battle axe Jinny",
Nivver said wi malice
  Fer Alice,
Tom, Dick, 'Arry
  An laal Jim
'Ull allus grin
  When we meet.
Neu Ah's retired
  It's a reeal treeat
Ti walk down t'street i' Millom.

XI SKEULIN

All t'lads an t'lasses
  Passed through t'classes
Of Gilling skeul.
  Joe Elliot towt wi a rule
Of iron.
  Miss Walton wooer "pince-nez" glasses
An' lurnt us lasses
  Sewin' an' knittin'.
Ah call ter mind sittin'
  On a varra 'ard form,
Mekkin' mittens ti keep t'sowjers warm,
  (Ah wur nobbut six).

Sittin' side bi side on t'lang desk,
  Wur an' uneeasy seeat fer conquest.
Forivver on t' 'op,
  Like Snakes an' Ladders,
At t'bottom or t'top
  Of t'class,
By gow, we wur restless.

Wurk wiped off t'slate
  Left no trace of t' 'ate
We ed fer sums an' spellin.
  Poitry we luved. Sir, tellin' t'tale of Oratius proud,
While we recited, "Rushing Lodore", aloud.

T'infants lurnt ter read t' 'ard way,
  They'd ter sing an' say,
C.A.T. cat, R.A.T. rat,
  But they lurnt reight weeal fer all that.
When it wur rainin' cats an' dogs,
  T'laal uns luved ter weear thur clogs.
Clitter clatter on t' 'ard steeans,
  T'rhythm wur ringin' i' thur bones.
They luved ter stamp an' mek gurt splashes,
  Weearin' thur shiny black goloshes.

At dinner time we roamed at will,
  Playing "Fox Off" away up t' 'ill
Of Gatherley Moor, wheear we fund
  T'early primrose close ter t'grund,
An' t'spot wheear grew
  T'fragrant violets white an' blue.
Up Jagger Lane, we fund
  T'fost bods' nests, "Foggy",
Fer t'blackie, spink, an spuggy.
  "Seccy", fer tom tit, throstle an t'cushat.
We climbed t' 'ollow tree ter peek at t'jenny 'ulat.

Ower t'dooer of t'blacksmith's shop
  We'd ing an' stop
Ter glooer at t'bellesis.
  T'shower o' sparks 'ud
Belch fra' t'smiddy fire.
  T' 'osses champed, an' varra recal
I' mi mind is stamped
  T'smell o' burning 'euf
An' t'iss of steam of a 'euped cart wheeal.

Then "Pitch Patch Pepper",
  Merrily we skipped our fill,
Laiked at "Itchy Bay" until
  T'whistle blew.

We've all scattered neu, an' med
  Our way i' uther parts.
Ah cam back ter bi wed.
  Mi muther an' mi father are at rest
In t'chochyard at Gilling West.
  'Appen t'best part
Is ter cum ageean, wi' a glad 'art,
  An' realise 'ut mebbe t'wisest
Larnin' was gitten fra' t'village
  An' t'skeulin, unwritten.

XII T'PIG AN CURRAN CEEAK

Yah beeakin' day
  Ah putten away
A curran' ceeak
  On t'dairy slab ter cool,
Fer it wur t'reul
  Nivver ter yut owt
Unless it wur cawd,
  An' awd.
Ah laited t'ceeak
  Mooer ner yance,
Fer t'next day's 'llowance.
  Ah leuked an' leuked in vain
But nivver clapped eyes on it ageean.
  T'mystery grew an' grew.
Noa gigantic mouse ner ratten
  Could ivver 'ev gitten
All t'lot down its throttle.
  Thur wur noa evidence
Of crumbs or currans.
  Varra soon t'Boss cam in,
Wi' a twinkle in 'is een,
  "Yan o' t'sews 'es gitten
An itch,
  Ah seed 'er scrat 'ersell soa much
She leusened t'sneck
  An oppened t'dairy dooer.
Ah'll bi bound
  She's been rowtin' reund an' reund
Ti finnd t'marra,
  Fer Ah deean't sarra
Pigs wi' curran ceeak.
  Now doan't chitter-chatter
An' fash thisell, Lass,
  'Appen t'currans
'll mek t'pig fatter!"

XIII WARTIME MEMORIES

"Cowton in the clay",
  Ah cam that way
Just a year o' mooer
  Afooer t'second world war.

Fooak try to fergit
  T'war an' all it browt
Afooer t'victory shout.
  I' them dark days
T'orkedest task
  Wes ti carry a gas mask.
T'Home Guard 'ud ask
  Who we wur an' wheear
We wur going.
  Just as though
They didn't knaw
  Us fra' Adam.

T' evacuees
  Cam fra t'Weear an' t'Tees
Ti t'village of East Cowton.
  Brothers, sisters, 'ugging parcels,
Carrying cases, laal morsels
  Of 'umanity.
They knew nowt abeut
  T'war ti be fowt
I' France, Africa an' Greece,
  Ner t'Browning gun, t'Radar screen
Ner t'submarine.
  Nobbut t'clutched Teddy Bear 'ud mean
Owt about t'life that 'ud been
  Safe at y'ham
Wi' Dad an' Mam.

"Ceukery van gingerbread".
  Ah tak a leuk i' mi ceukery beuk,
Ti see how we med
  All mak o' wartime dishes
I' t'laal van,
  Wi' tinned fishes,
Dried egg, ertsatz sossidge.
  "Dig fer Victory", was Churchill's message.
T'farmers grund
  Wheeat an' med a pund
O' two o' meeal
  Fer breead.
That wur a reeal treeat.

T'air-raid warden
  On 'is beat,
Used ti showt ower t'garden
  Wall, "Put eut that leet,
Jerry's bombs 'll fall terneet."
  T'bomber's aim wern't true,
An' afooer we knew,
  A Molotov Cocktail ed dropped
Askew i' Miller's staggarth.
  Awd Tom in a frenzy popped
T'en meeal on t'top an' stopped
  T'girt blaze.
He knew 'ow ti guard
  'Is pigs an' 'ens an' ration card.

T'farmers ed ti grow mooer corn,
  An' varra seun wer worn
Eut wi wark.
  T'sowjers 'elped 'em monny a day,
Stookin' corn, tonnin' 'ay,
  Cuttin' banns on thrashin' day,
Howin' tunnups, leukin' thistles,
  Gearin' t' 'osses, 'earin'

T'missel thrush
  Fair brossen wi singin,
In t'bawtree bush.
  They'd scrat taties, spreead muck,
An' teuk ti t'land
  Like ducks ti t'watter.
An' varra seun forgot t'clatter
  Of t'tanks, t'wail
Of t'siren an' t'thud o' t'guns.
  Cowton air
'Ed 'elped ti reight t'wrangs,
  An' in t'feight
Ed 'appen 'elped ti put t' world reight.

* In 1940 senior village girls had Domestic Science lessons in a large mobile van, "The Ceukery Van". At the beginning of the war "The Ceukery Van" teacher instructed village housewives in wartime cookery.

XIV T'BUFFET SUPPER

Cheers! A cockteeal?
  Ah've nivver seed
Owt like this.
  It leuks like pond watter,
Wi' bits o' green matter
  Like weed
Flooatin' on t'top.
  Ah moan't ton mi back
Lest
  T'ostess 'll cop
Mi tippin' all t'lot
  Inter t'pot
Of t'floral decoration.
  Thur'd be sike
A noration
  As nivver was.

Nowadays
  T'modern way's
Ti 'ev t'grub
  Spreead eut on t'teeable.
Yer able
  Ti 'elp yersell.
Yer can 'ardlins tell
  What ti choose
Thur's sike queues.

We 'ev a chin wag,
  "Ah wunder if shu knaws
Ut Ah think 'ur poncho's
  Nobbut a cagmag."

Thur's gossip an' talk
  "Is it 'am, 'en, or pork?"
Ah think
  Ah cud put all t'lot
I mi ee an wink.

Ah can ken
  T'sossidge roll, an' savour
T'flavour
  Of a curlycue of peeastry
That's teeasty.

On yon dish
  Thur's summat like fish,
An bits o' cawd tooast
  Like leather.
Ah wunder whether
  Thur topped eut
Wi cheese or eggs.

By gum, mi legs is bad
  Thur's noa chairs
Soa Ah'll etter sit
  Misell deun on t'stairs.

XV DIGGIN

Yus Ah've been diggin,
  Nut in t'gardin or in t'midden
Tekkin a gurt swipe
  Wi a fower tined gripe,
But at Vindolanda
  Away up in Northumbria.
We wur leukin fer brass,
  Pots an sike like
Ut t'Romans lost,
  Mebbe tossed
Aside
  Two thousand yeears sin.

Fooak ud pass,
  Ceus an sheep ud yut grass
  An nivver knaw
Of t'treasure apped up
  An felted in t'grund belaw.

Neu yah cawd misly day
  We fun our way
Ter t'Roman site,
  Dug wi might an main
In Northumbria's wind and rain.
  Crouchin, kneelin,
Bendin, liggin,
  Scrattin in t'clay and t'sand
Tekkin t'trouble
  Ter leuk ut ivvery speck o' rubble.

We'd "Diggin Fever".
  An ud gently lever
A gurt steean,
  Leukin wi starin een,
Ter finnd a bit o' ceukin
  Pot or a rusty nail.

Peggy fund leaden bullets
  Big an white as 'ulat's eggs.
Janet spied some brass in t'clay
  Wi t'eead of t'Boss
Severus as plain as day.

Mi back fair warked,
  Mi fingers wur stiff
Soa Ah weshed t'pots,
  Scrubbin em cleean
Soa all t'marks cud be clearly seen.
  Ah fun a bit
Wi a gallopin beease on it,
  Mebbe a bull
Ut ed gitten eut of its ull.

T'day passed
  Bent double
In t'trench,
  Fergittin' all worry and trouble
Tryin' ter finnd t'answer
  Ter t'Roman riddle.

XVI T'BEEAT GROUP

Neeamed "Thunner an' Lightnin",
  T'beeat group
Leuked quite frightenin'
  Wi' thur flounces an' frills,
Warbles an' trills,
  An' seund that bounced
Back ageean.

T'lads rocked
  An' tremmled,
Like dithery docks.
  Mini wur t'lasses' dresses,
Maxi wur t'drummer's tresses,
  Which leuked mooer like wisps of 'ay.
(Ah dasn't say
  Like ratten teeals),
Fer t'modern males
  'Appen leuk older,
Think thur wiser, bolder,
  Wi' 'air deun on thur showlder.

A sudden gurt bang,
  Med mi wunder whativver wur wrang,
Fer t'timpani
  Wekkened up t'company,
Ti anuther gurt creunin',
  Gurnin', sweunin'
Session,
  A confession
Of Luv!

Ah mooan't condemn
  These modern men.
In eur young days,
  We had new-fanguld ways
Of dancin' t'Charleston, t'Tango.
  Mi mother thowt Ah wur mad
Ti git mi 'air cropped
  Like a lad.
T'men fooak wur reight pleased
  That eur frocks covered eur knees.
Soa t'circle's completed,
  An' eur condemnation,
Defeated.

XVII T'LAUND–ER–ETTE

Eight gleamin wesh tubs
  Sit side bi side.
Thur's nobs an screws
  Ter use,
An brass ti pay,
  T'new fanguld way.

Ah sam mi close
  An brass in.
Thur's sike a din.
  T'weshin's 'uzzockin up an deun,
In a crazy fashion.

T'red leet's flashin!

T'new contraption's
  Ed a tiff.
It's in a 'uff,
  An stopped its jigglin motion.
Ah've a fit,
  Fer Ah've a notion
Ut Ah've brokken it.

A laal lass sez
  "Thoo's sammed thi close in wrang."
Soa Ah prod amang
  T'weshin,
An seun t'sossin an t'splashin
  Starts all ower ageean.

Thur's nowt to deu
  Noa peace
Ner room fer elbow grease.
  We sit an chat
Abeut this an that.
  T'bairns laik.
Ah tek a nap,
  An dreeam
Of possin tubs,
  T'set pot
An t'smell o' yat
  Soap suds,
Peggy sticks,
  Dolly legs
An gipsy pegs,
  An cleean fergit
T'Laund-er-ette.

But t'job's nut done.
  Ah mun
Dry mi weshin
  T'modern way,
Fer it's nobbut a misty, misly day.
  Insteead o' proppin
T'cloase 'igher,
  Soa thu'll flap wi ease
In t'gentle breeze,
  Thu mun play Tig,
Reund an reund,
  In t'whirligig
Of t'tumble air drier.

A notice sez
  "Don't fowld yer cloase
In 'ere, leave reum
  Fer t'uthers."

Soa, we mun go
  Eutside inter t'Markit Square.
By gum, fooak don't awf stan an stare
  At two awd muthers
Fowldin t'sheet.
  In t'street.
"Put a move on, Jane"
  Sez Molly,
"Fer t'rain's set in,
  An t'weshin's
Gettin wet,
  Eutside
T'Launder-er-ette!"

XVIII

THOWTS AFTER A PAIN MANAGEMENT COURSE *
AT WALTON HOSPITAL, LIVERPOOL. JUNE 1985

All mak o' quaks,
  Acupuncturists,
Cranial osteopathists,
  An off beat 'acks
Ev ed a go at me.
  Ah've been kept on t'op
Oppened mi lugs
  Ter t'top
Specialists ut Barra' an' Charin' Cross.
  Ah'd speculate an accumulate
Reasons. WHY? OH WHY?

Ah'd notions
  Ut pills an' potions
Wad cure me.
  Physic bi t'bottle
  Es gone deun mi throttle.
Tongue twistin' neeams
  Ffluffenamide, clomipramine
Molipraxine
  Wur like songs ter bi sung
As thu' rolled off t'Doctor's tongue.
  (Thu did nowt fer me).

* An attempt to tolerate a constant facial pain!

New yah day
  Ah fun summat eut
Abeut PAIN.
  (On t'wireless).
Thu' wur a noration
  An' information.
Noa magic wand or instant cure
  But Ah wur sure
Ut medics fra
  Bradford, Kidderminster or Liverpool,
Wad nut feul
  Abeut wi' me.

Soa Ah cam ter see Dr. Wells
  Who tells me
"Thu's no cure
  Yer mun elp yursell."
In June
  Ah cam ter room
Nine, Cairns Ward.
  Fer t'ole month
Ah nivver wus bored.
  Ellen, Melanie, Sue, Esther,
Liz, Linda, Jean, Debbie,
  Eric an' Dr Wells ev talked.

Ah've walked
  Tall.
Ah've danced
  Swum in t'watter.
Ed monny a natter
  Relaxed, kept fit
Asked questions
  Said mi bit
Felt free.
  (An Ah's seventy three).

XIX MI TARGETS

Ah'll go ter Preston an' git mi degree.
  Ah'll mebbe nut skip, ner cycle
But mi gran' dawters'll remember me,
  An able Grandma
Nut a vegetable.
  Wi deep breathin'
Ah mun blow eut eighty cannels
  On mi bothday cake
Nivver showin' a pain ner an ache.

Jane Horner Smith
Millom, Cumbria.

GLOSSARY

'ap up	– give cattle bedding
'ay moo	– space above byre for hay to be stored
'ind	– hind, agricultural worker
'llowance	– ten o' clock, coffee break
'ull	– farm building for animals
Ah	– I
a'brimmin	– in season
addle	– to earn
all mak o'	– all kinds of
allus	– always
awm	– elm
bands	– straw bands to secure sheaves of corn
bawtree	– elderberry
beease	– beast, farm animal
beease	– cattle
bellesis	– bellows
blackie	– blackbird
brass	– money
brokken	– broken
brossen	– bursting
cagmag	– worn out item (clothes)
cauf	– calf
cawd	– cold
chippin'	– hatching
cleut	– clout, wallop, hit
clocker	– a broody hen
clout	– a cloth
clutch	– young ones, chickens
cocks	– haycocks
ceu	– cow
creddle	– cradle
cushat	– wood pigeon
cutter bar	– grass cutter bar
Dolly legs	– stool-like posser used in rotary movement
dab 'and	– skilled
dicky	– not very well
dithery docks	– quaking grass
een	– eyes, (pl. of "ee")

effer	– heifer
esh	– ash
etter	– have to
euped	– hooped
euse	– persistent cough
fellies	– fellows, curved part, circumference of wheel
felted	– hidden
fettle	– to make all right
finnd	– find
flig	– to go away, as young birds leave the nest
foggy	– the first
fratch	– be at odds with everything
fun, fund	– found
gallowa'	– a Dales pony
geslins	– goslings
girss	– grass
gitten	– got
gurnin'	– pulling strange faces
gurt	– big
howin	– hoeing
Itchy bay	– hopscotch
ilk	– kind
in a 'uff	– take umbrage
ing	– hang
jenny ulet	– owl
kist	– chest
kitchen press	– combined cupboard and chest of drawers
kittlin	– kitten
laal	– little
laikin	– playing
laited	– looked for
leukin' thistles	– cutting thistles with a narrow hoe (looker)
liggin	– lying
lonnin	– lane
lowse eut	– to take the harness off a horse
lug-carry	
March 'ares	– hares boxing each other
marra	– the 'other one' of a pair
mawk	– to kill the eggs laid by blow flies on sheep
misly	– rainy, drizzly

mun	– must
naff	– hub of wheel
nobbut	– only
noration	– rumpus, row
oose	– a cough
oppenin eut	– a path is made by hand so the binder can start
ower thrang	– too busy
owt	– anything
pancheon	– large earthen ware bowl
Peggy stick	– a posser for use in a wooden tub
peltin	– throwing
plooat	– ploat, pluck feathers
pund	– pound
putten	– put
ratten	– rat
sammed	– pushed
sarra	– to feed animals
scrat taties	– pick, harvest potatoes
scrat	– to work hard
seccy	– second
seed	– seen
set pot	– copper for boiling washing
sew	– a sow (pig)
sile	– to strain
smiddy	– blacksmith's shop. The blacksmith shod horses and put hoops on wheels
socks	– the sharp end, point of a plough
spink	– bullfinch
spuggy	– sparrow
staggarth	– stackyard
steg	– gander
stell	– a wide drainage ditch
stob	– quill end of a feather
t'ceu's springin	– the cow will calve soon
t'easins	– maximum extent of a stack
t'rain's set in	– a continuous downpour
tan	– to beat, hit
teeafit	– peewit
tekken	– taken
teuk 'er ook	– went away

thoo, thou	– "you", familiar form of address
throstle	– thrush
throttle	– throat
thunner	– thunder
togs	– clothes
tunnin 'ay	– turning hay with a hand rake
topped eut	– finishing off the top of a haysack
towt	– taught
tunnup	– turnip
wall-eyed	– one brown eye and one blue eye
wark	– to ache
watter	– water
witter	– guinea fowl
woosit	– worsted
y'ham	– home
yackers	– acres
yah	– one
yak	– oak
yance	– once
yat	– hot
yuster	– used to
yut	– to eat